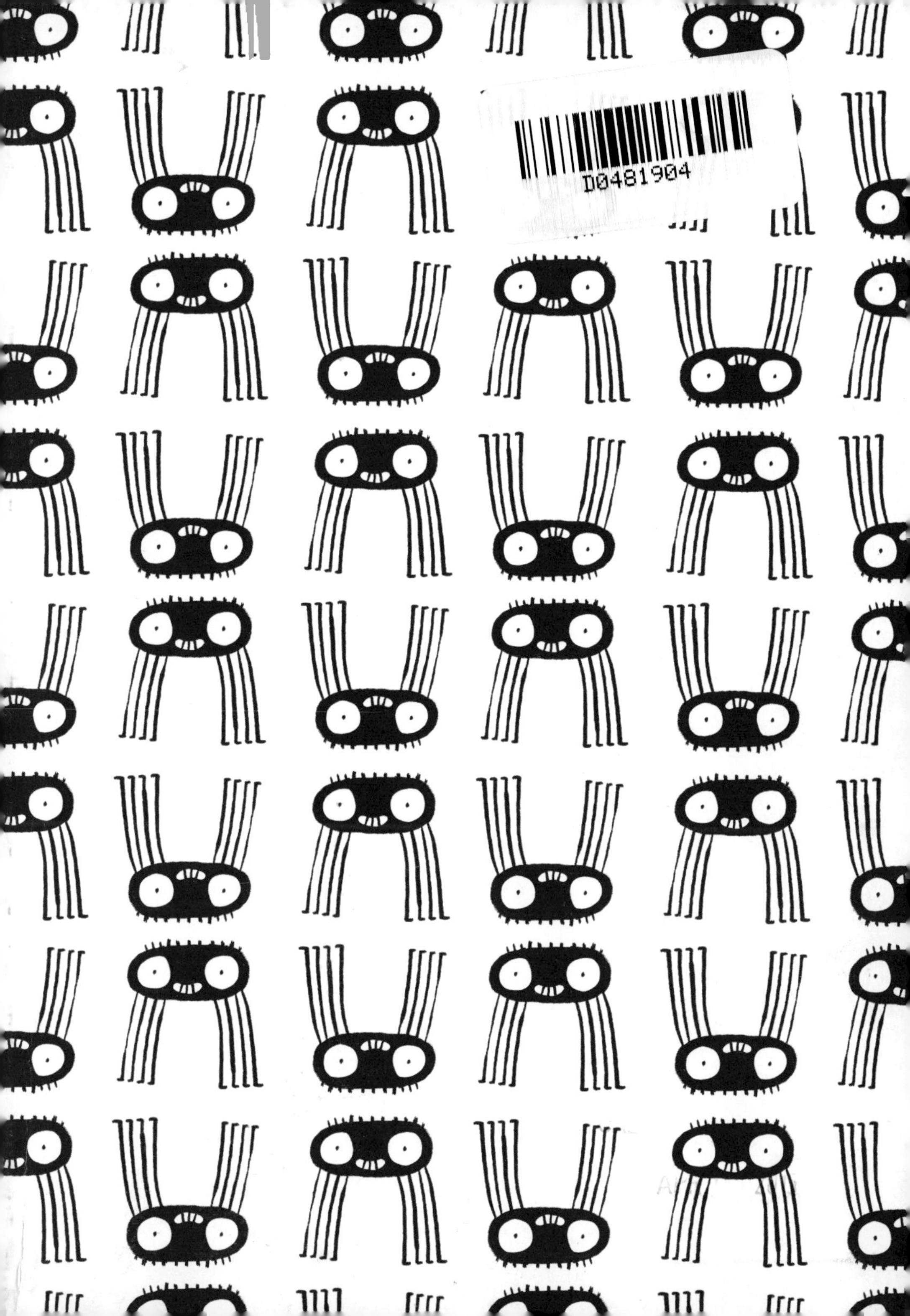

THE SPIDER

For Emma,
who, like the spider, is not an insect

Originally published as *L'araignée* by Les éditions de la courte échelle inc.

Copyright © 2015 Elise Gravel
Copyright for the French edition: Elise Gravel and Les éditions de la courte échelle inc., 2014

Published in Canada by Tundra Books, a division of Random House of Canada Limited,
One Toronto Street, Suite 300, Toronto, Ontario M5C 2V6

Published in the United States by Tundra Books of Northern New York,
P.O. Box 1030, Plattsburgh, New York 12901

Library of Congress Control Number: 2014941839

Library and Archives Canada Cataloguing in Publication

Gravel, Elise
[Araignée. English]
        The spider / written and illustrated by Elise Gravel.

(Disgusting critters)
Translation of: L'araignée.
Issued in print and electronic formats.
ISBN 978-1-77049-664-4 (bound).—ISBN 978-1-77049-666-8 (epub)

        I. Spiders—Juvenile literature. I. Title. II. Title: Araignée. English.

QL458.4.G7213 2015   j595.4'4   C2014-903065-7
                                          C2014-903066-5

English edition edited by Samantha Swenson
Designed by Elise Gravel and Tundra Books
The artwork in this book was rendered digitally.

www.tundrabooks.com

Printed and bound in China

1 2 3 4 5 6   20 19 18 17 16 15

Elise Gravel

THE SPIDER

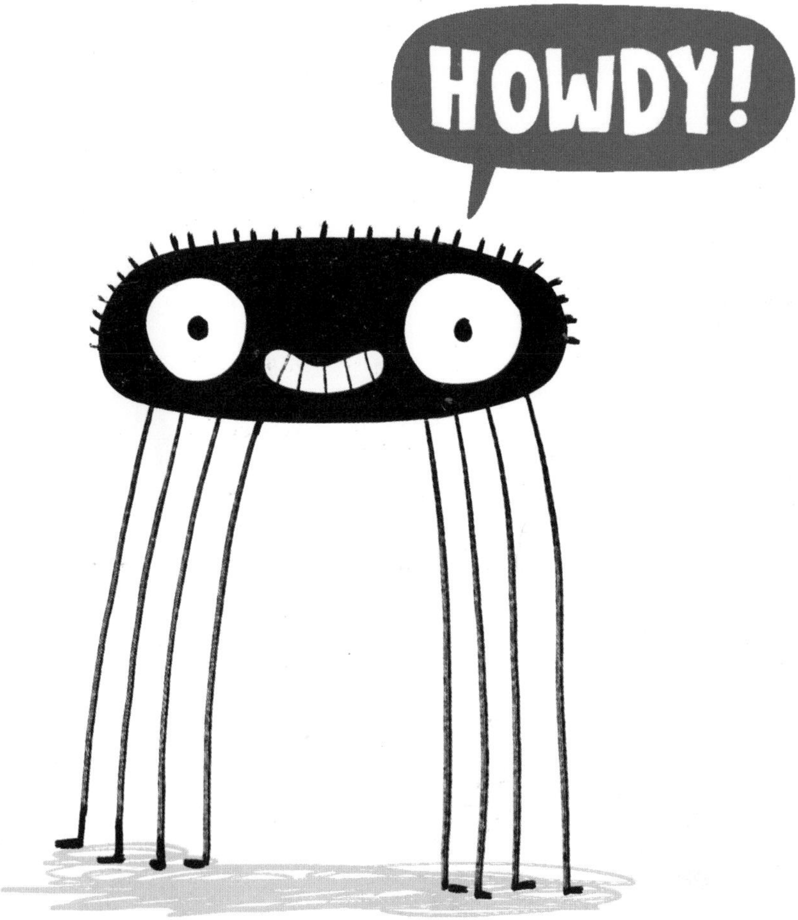
HOWDY!

Tundra Books

Ladies and gentlemen, please welcome
your friend

THE SPIDER.

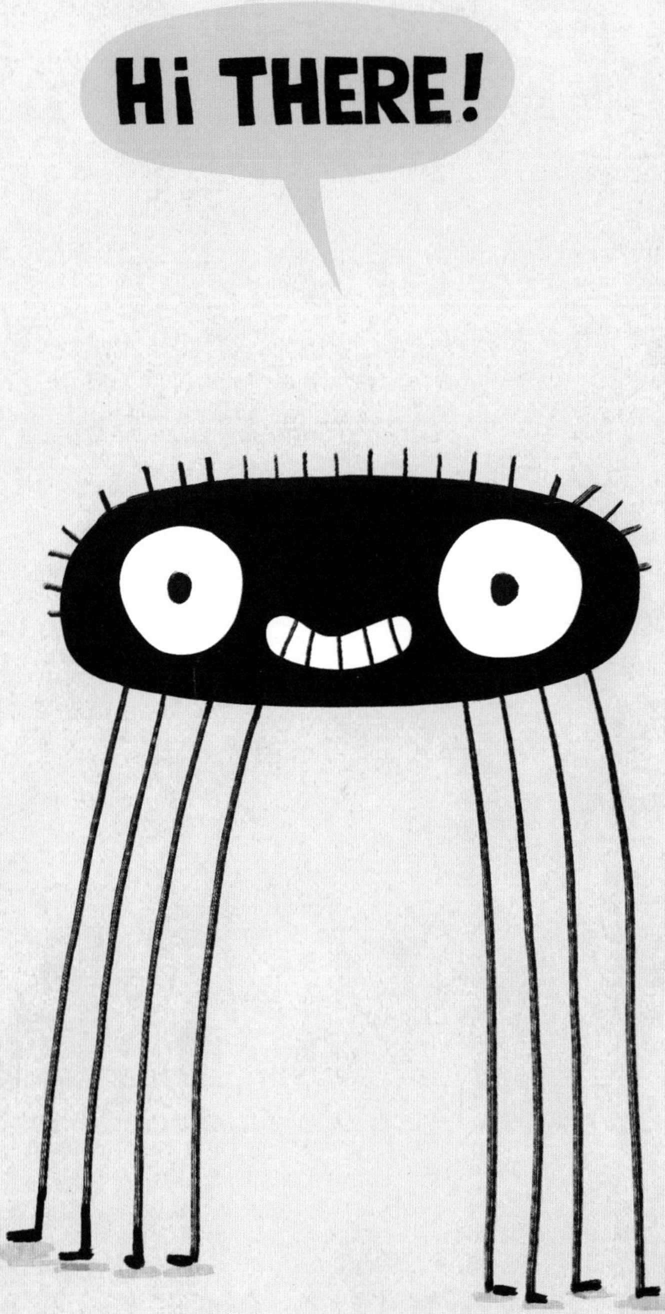
Hi THERE!

There are over 40,000 species of spiders. They can live in almost any environment:

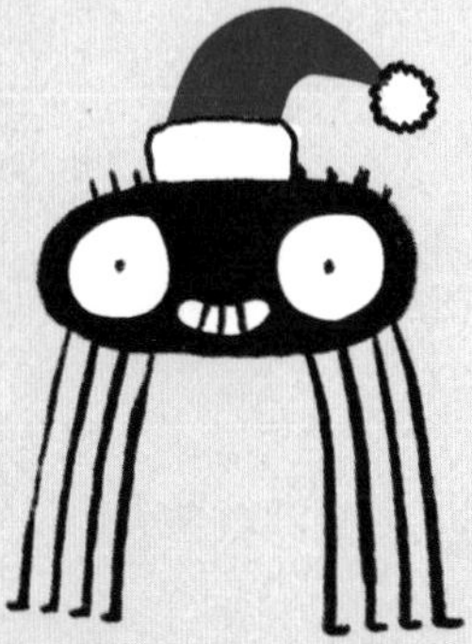

In cold climates

In warm climates

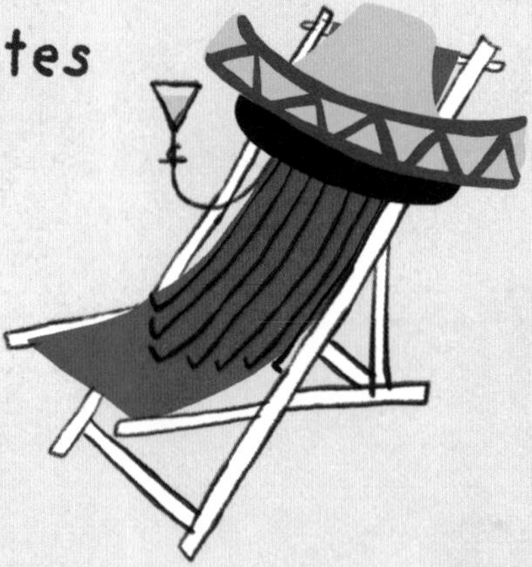

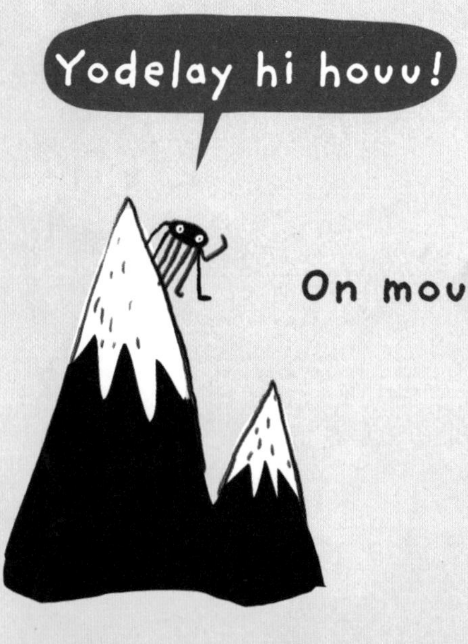
Yodelay hi houu!

On mountaintops

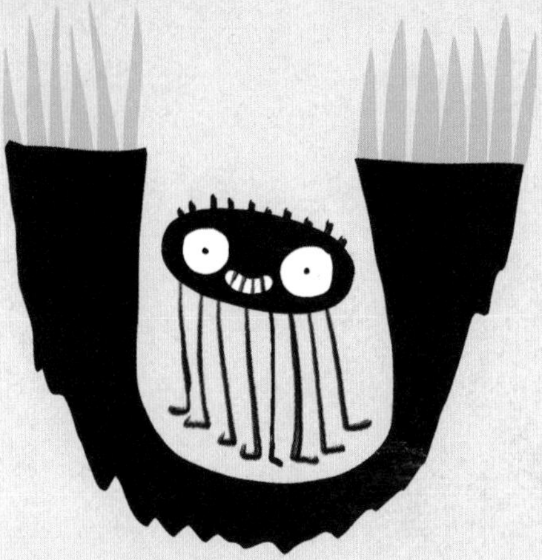

Underground

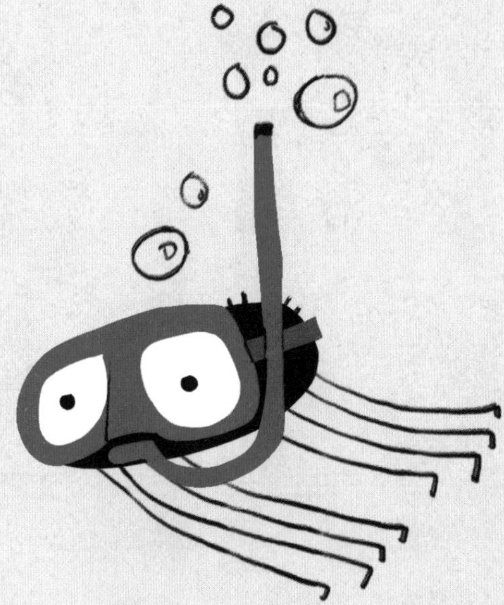

Underwater

. . . But not in outer space.

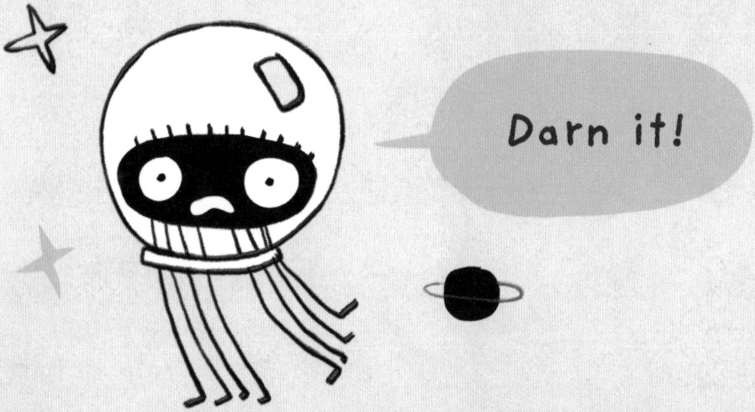
Darn it!

Since she has eight legs, the spider is not considered an

iNSECT.

Insects only have six legs.

Maybe not, but I'm so pretty in princess shoes.

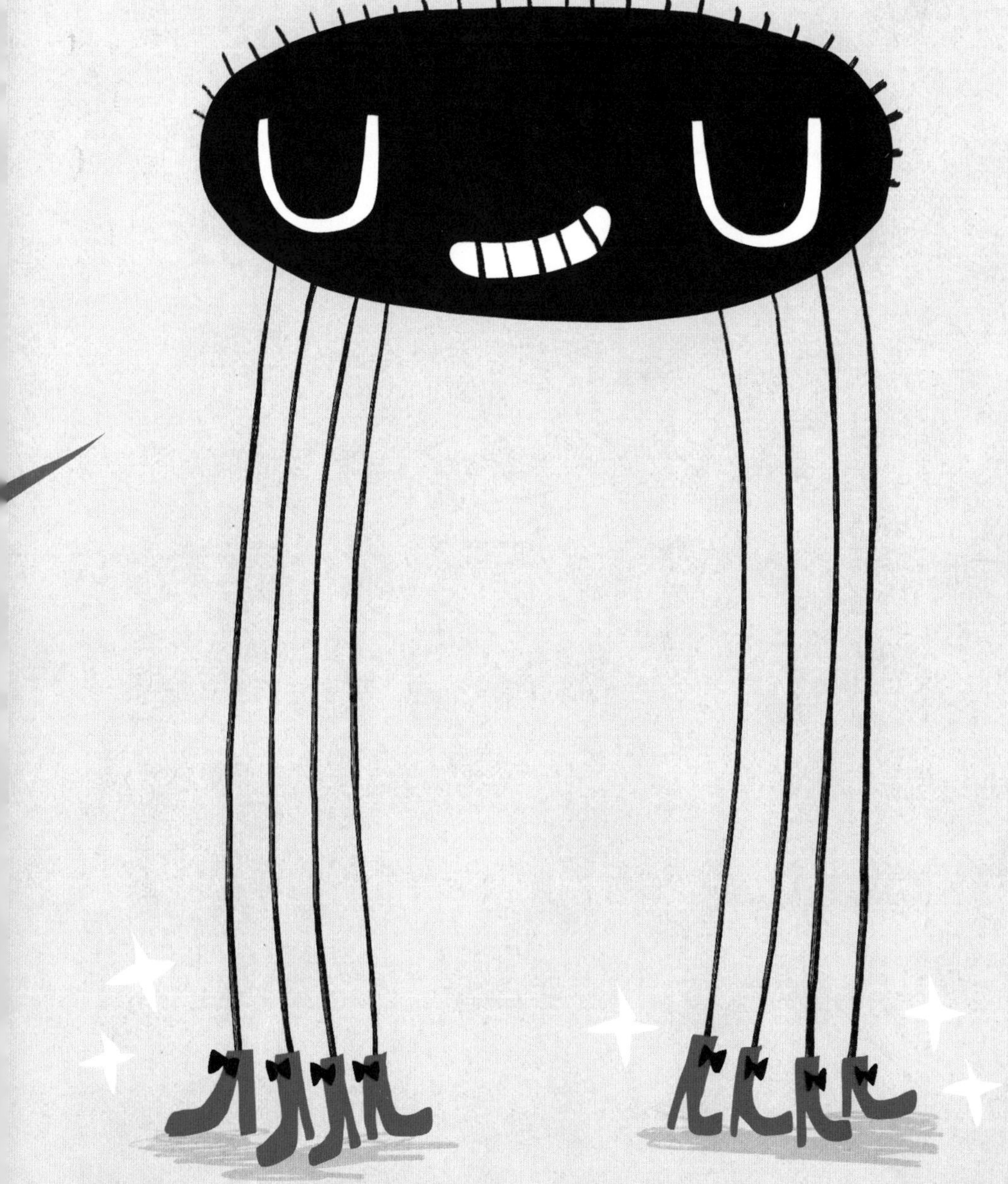

Most spiders have poisonous fangs in their mouths and

FOUR PAIRS OF EYES.

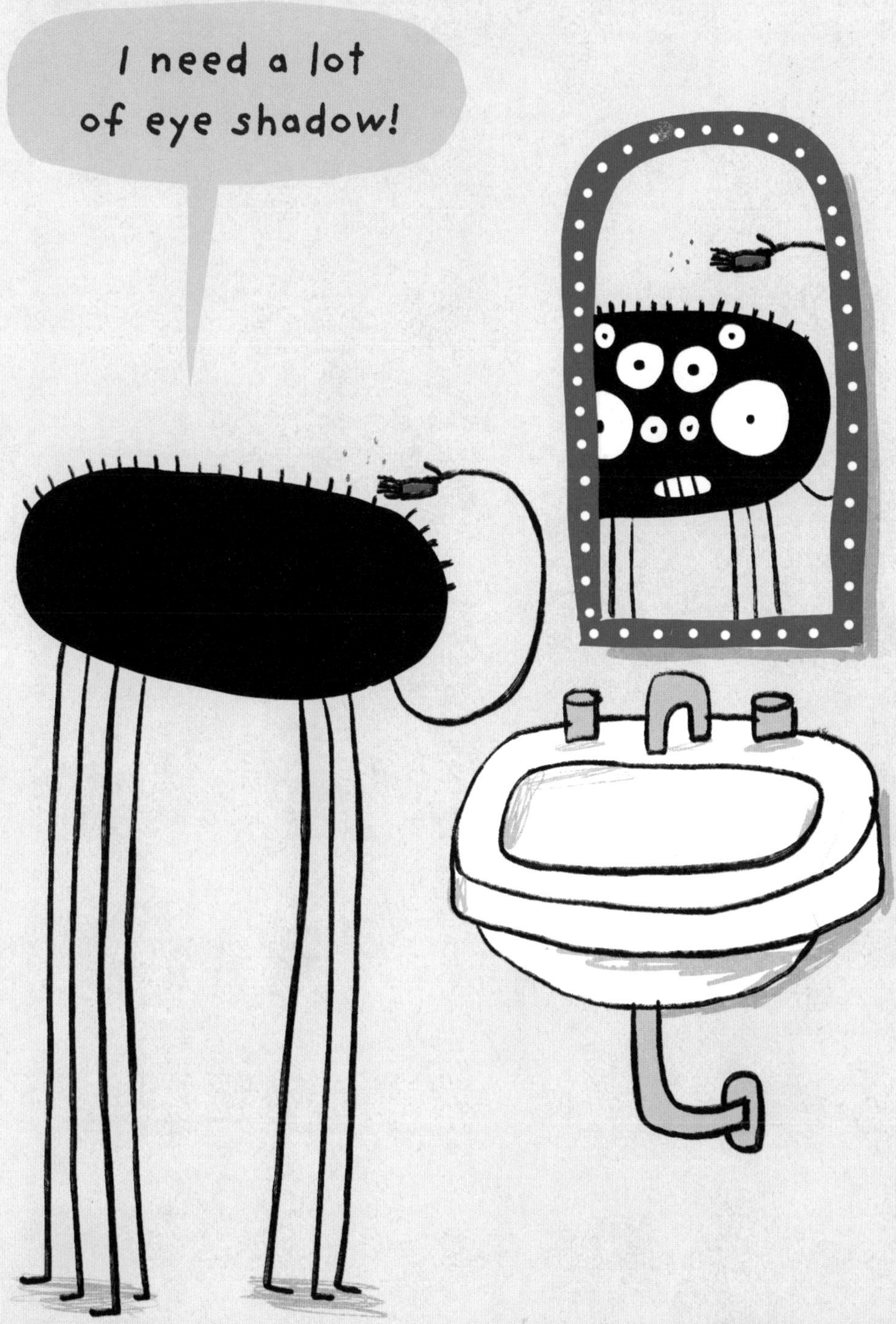
I need a lot of eye shadow!

Spiders produce

SiLK

with their abdomens.

Their silk can be used
for many things:

to build webs

ooOYOYooo
OOOOOOO!

as a means of
transportation

to protect their eggs

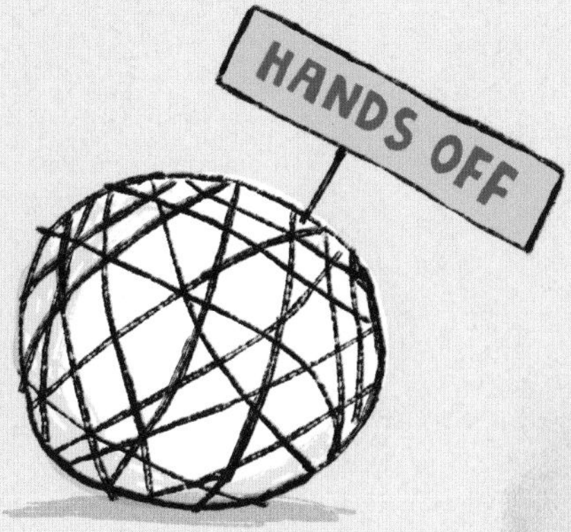
HANDS OFF

to create webs that trap air so they can breathe underwater.

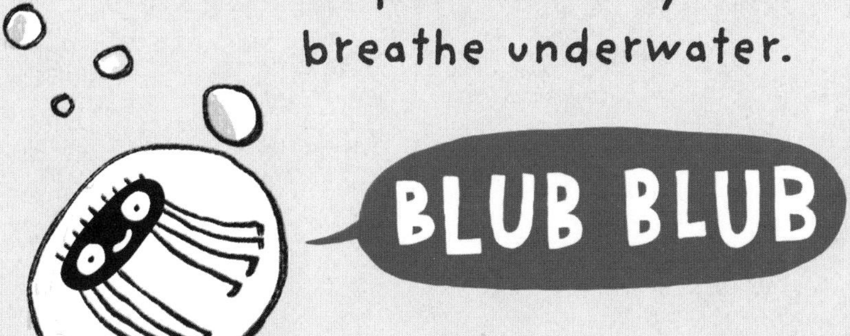
BLUB BLUB

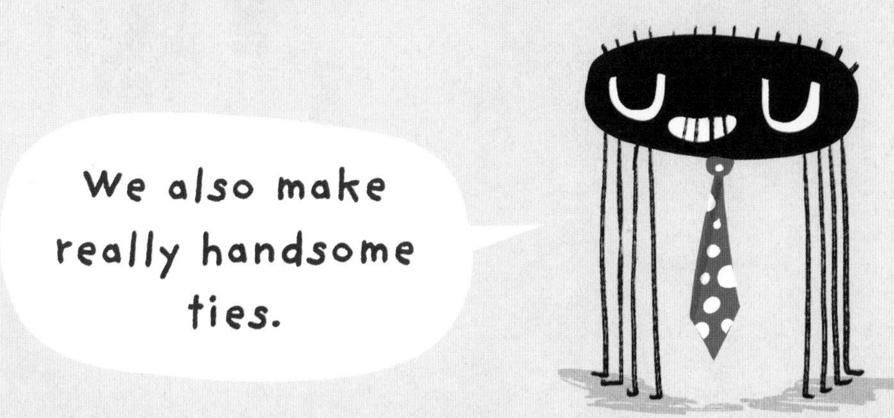
We also make really handsome ties.

Spiders mostly eat other insects. They have many different ways of catching their prey: some use a sticky net as a trap, others jump on their prey and some catch their prey with a

LASSO.

YEEHAW!

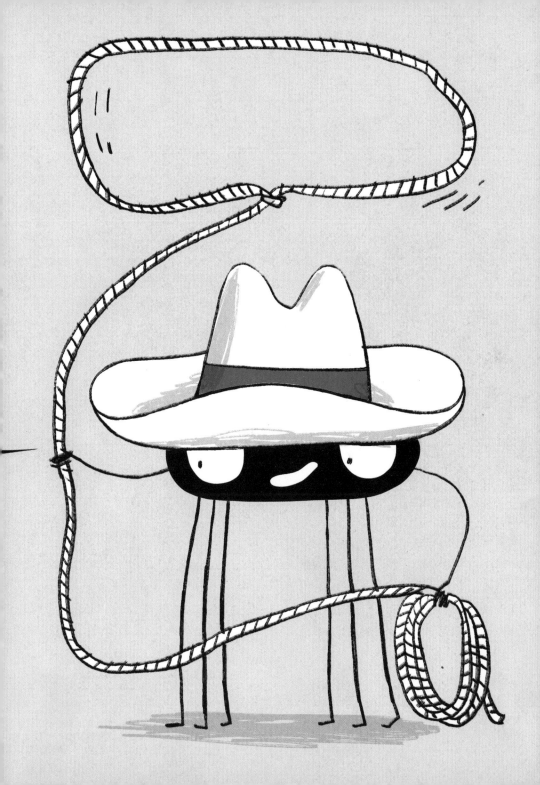

Some spiders even

MiMiC

their prey to make it easier to sneak up on them.

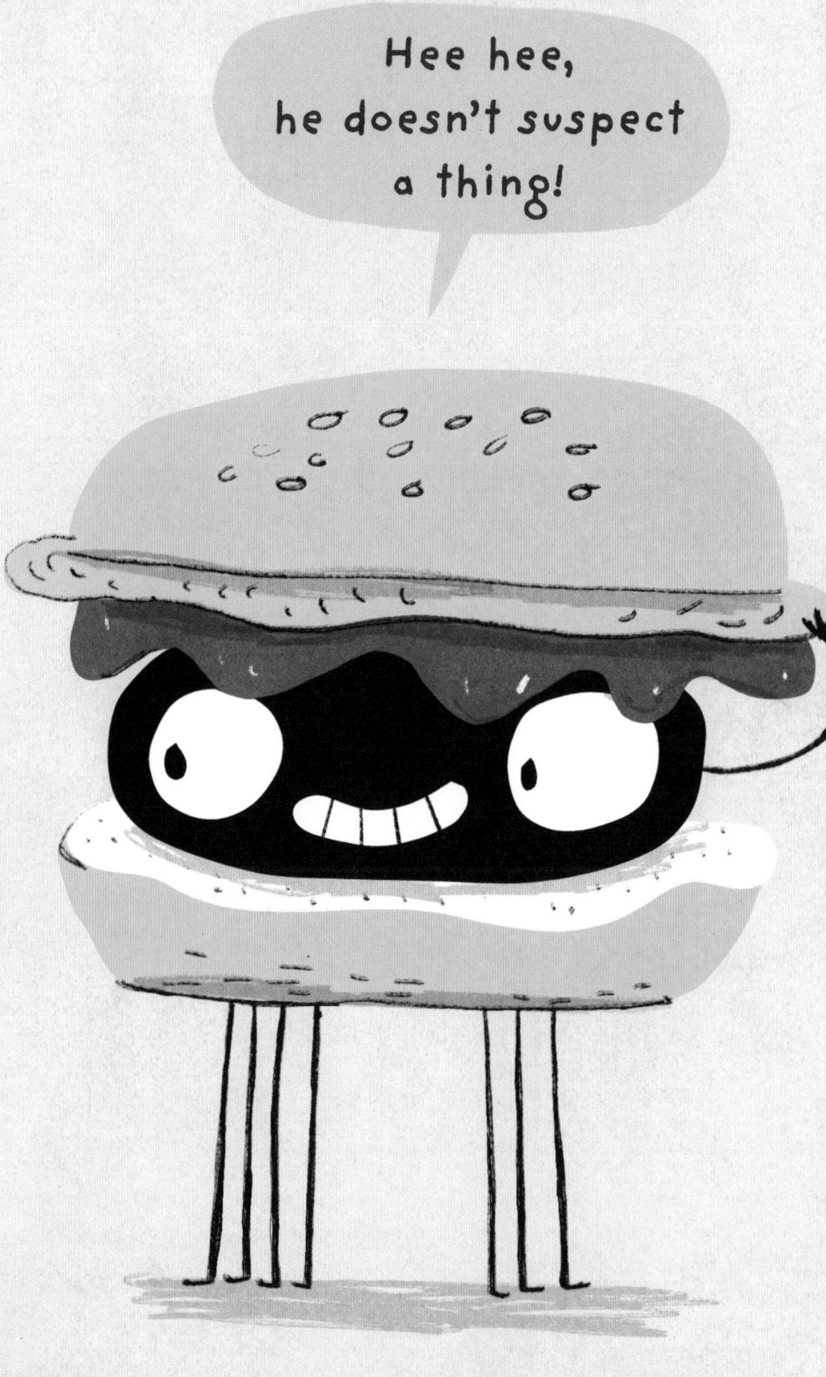
Hee hee, he doesn't suspect a thing!

In many spider species, the

FEMALE

is bigger than the

MALE.

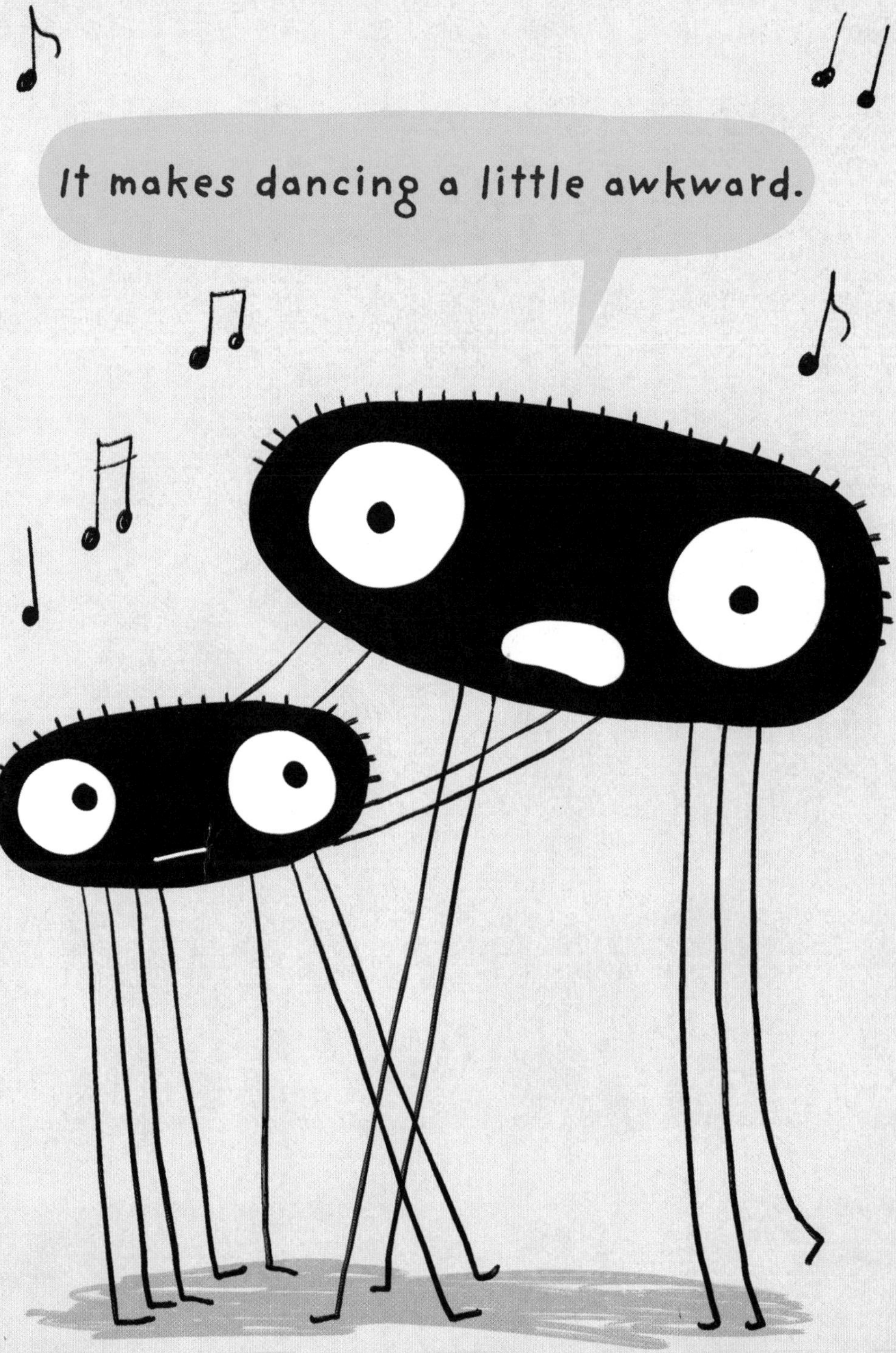
It makes dancing a little awkward.

After some spiders mate, the female spider will

EAT THE MALE.

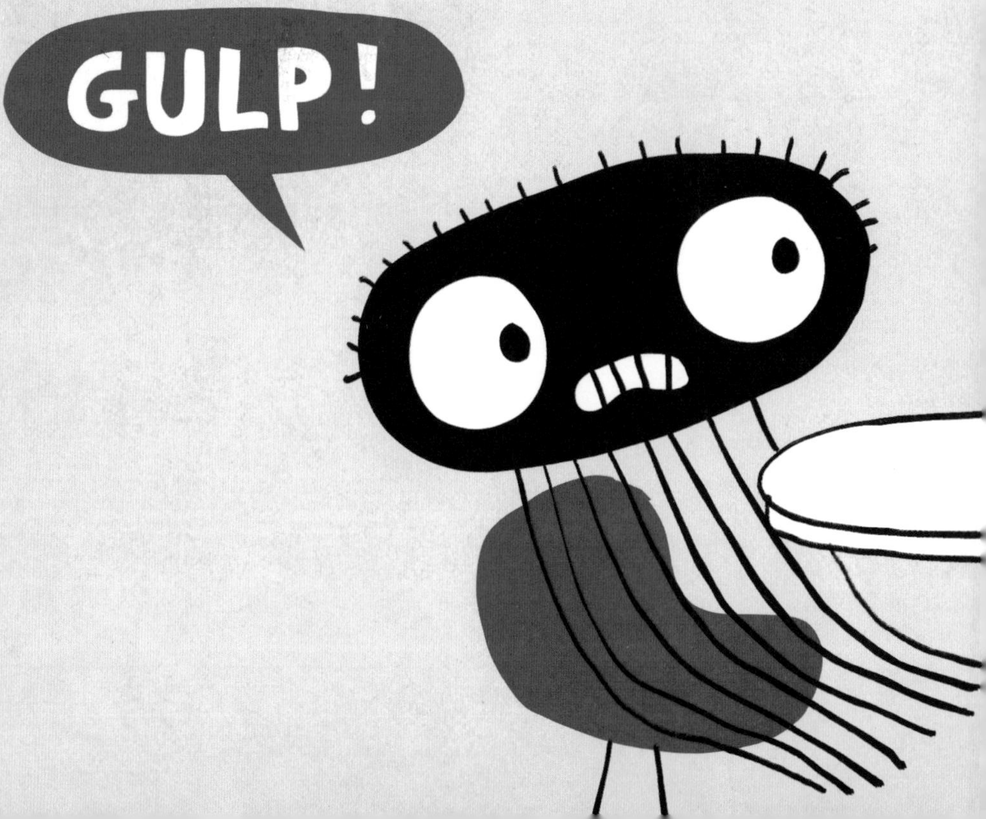
GULP!

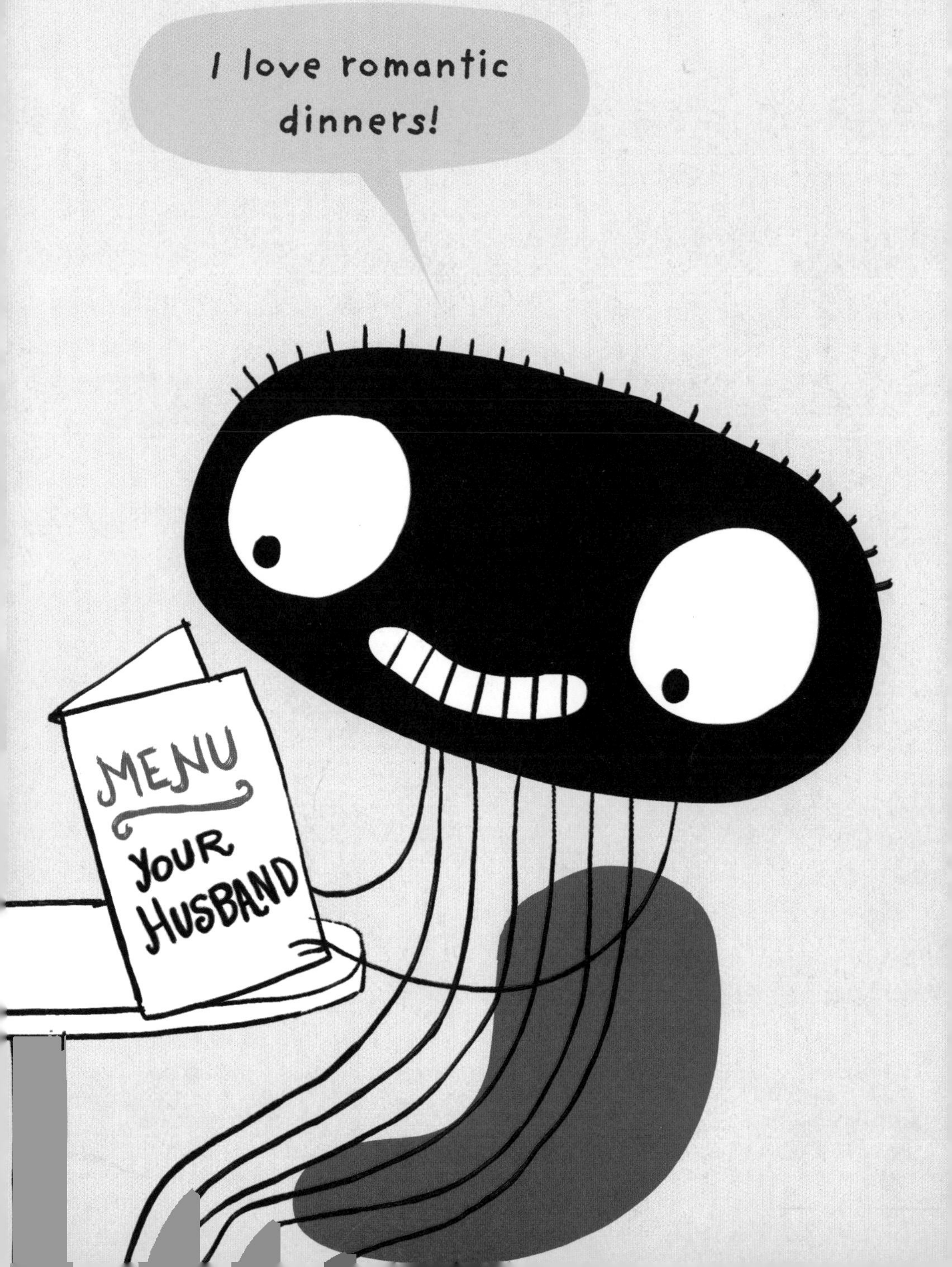
I love romantic dinners!
MENU
YOUR HUSBAND

The female spider can lay up to a thousand

EGGS.

She wraps them up in her silk and carries them around with her.

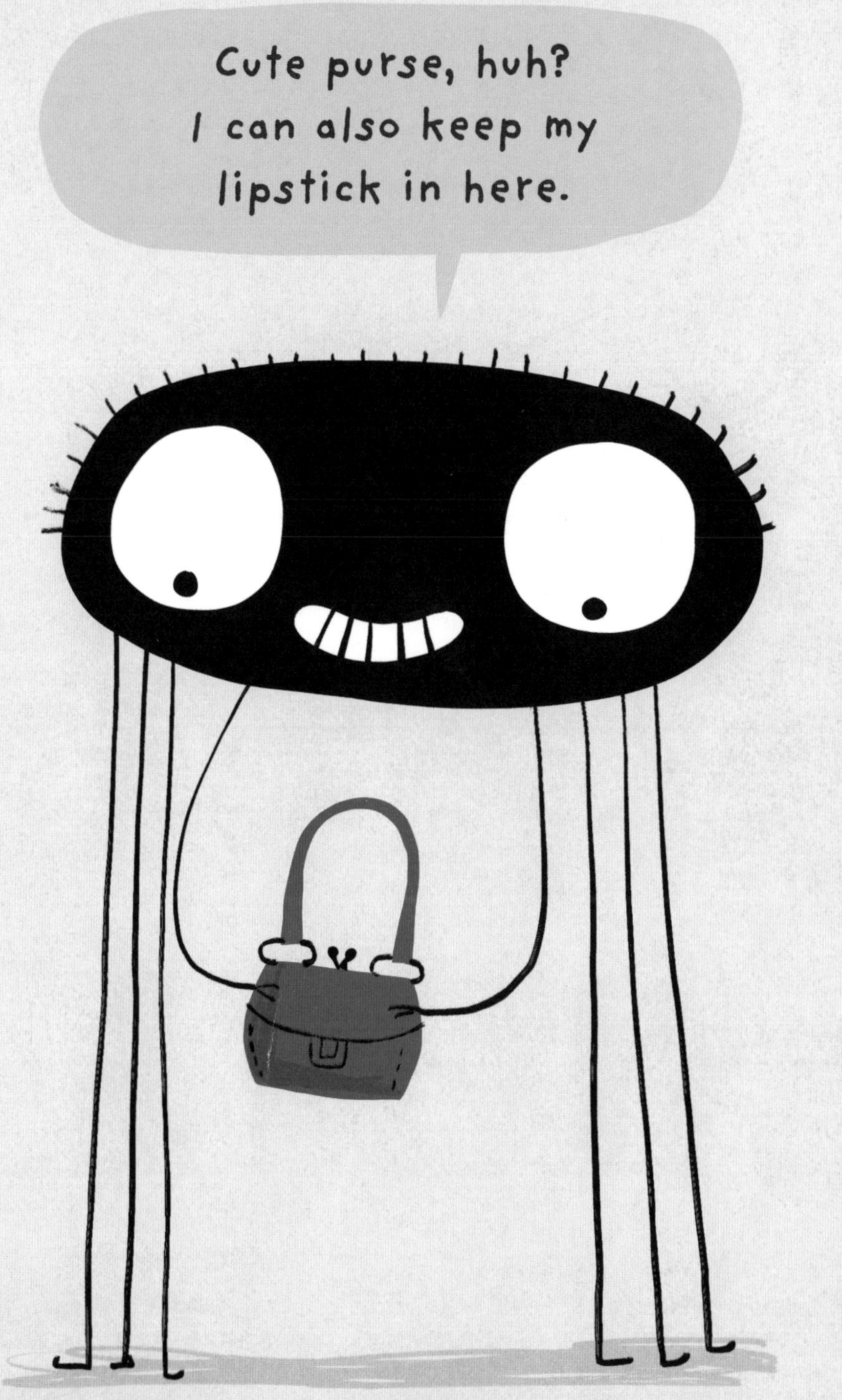
Cute purse, huh? I can also keep my lipstick in here.

Some mothers carry the baby spiders

ON THEIR BACKS

until the babies are old enough to

DEFEND

themselves.

Are we there yet?

Are we there yet?

Are we there yet?

People are often afraid of spiders, but most spiders are

NOT DANGEROUS

to humans. In fact, spiders have much more reason to be scared of us!

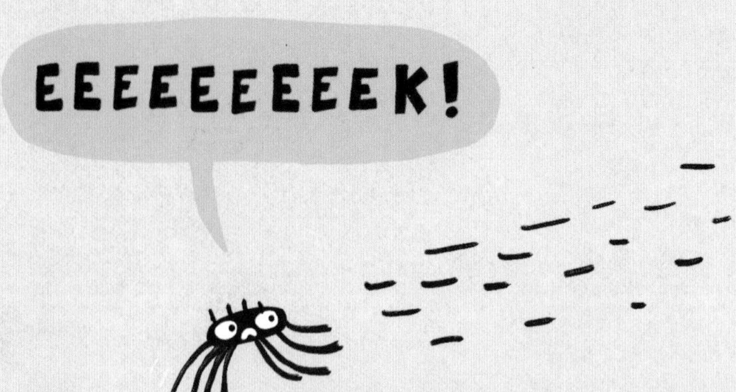
EEEEEEEEEEK!

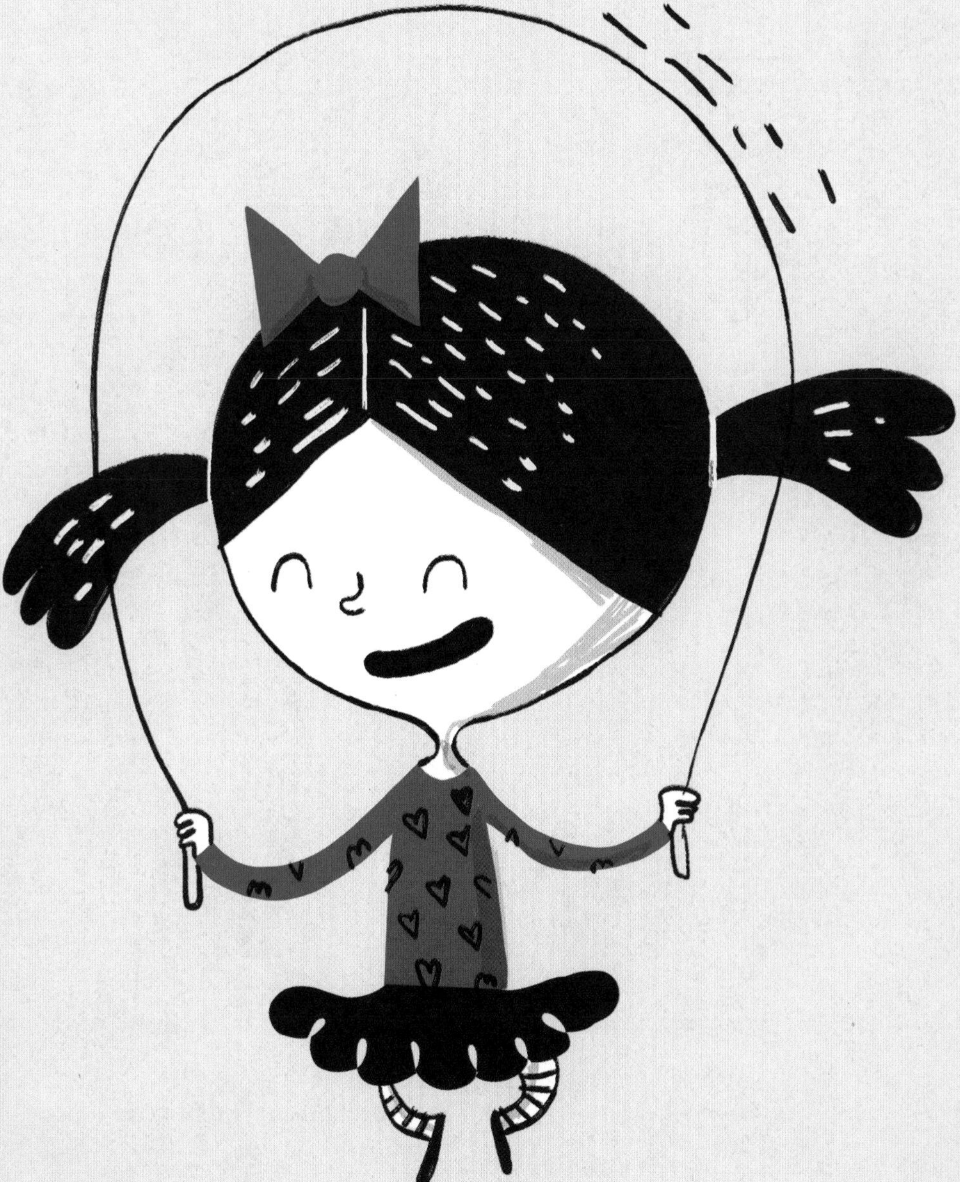

The spider can be helpful. Since she eats other

INSECTS,

she can get rid of annoying ones like mosquitoes and flies.

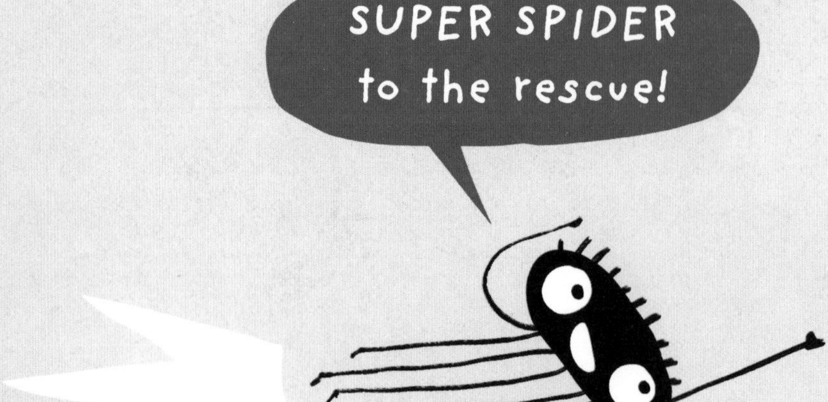
SUPER SPIDER
to the rescue!

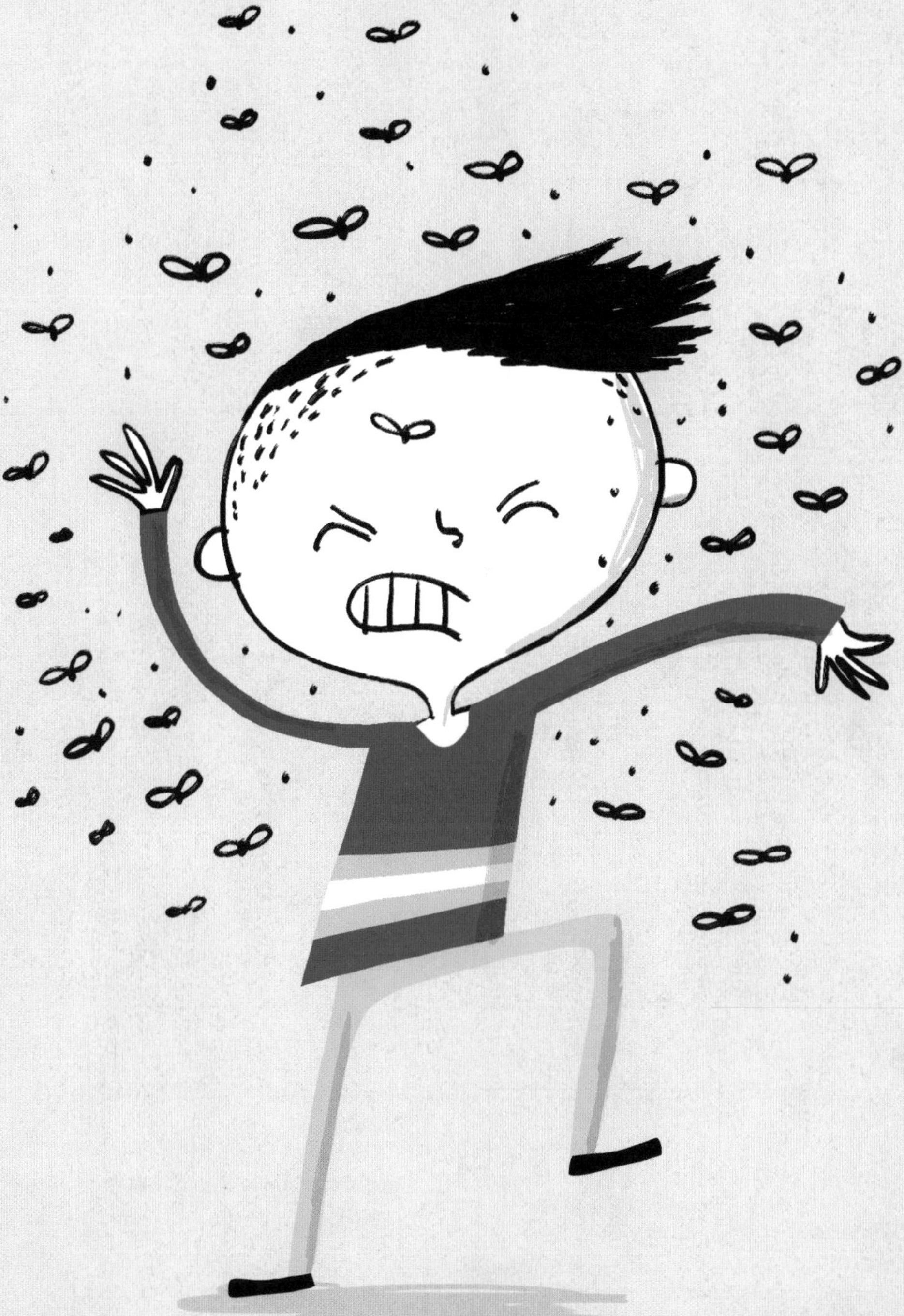

So the next time you meet a spider, shake her

HAND!

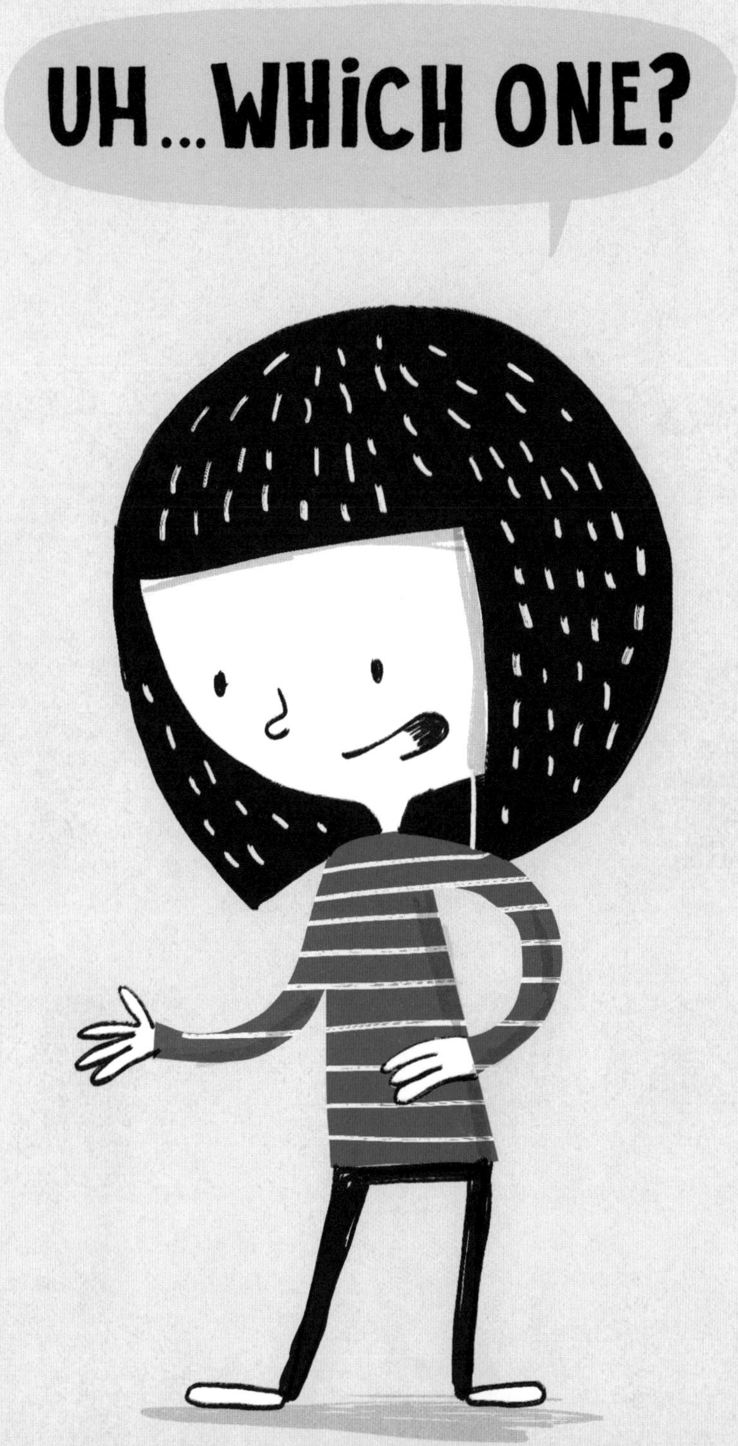
UH...WHICH ONE?